GARBH SANSKARA

A Complete Guide of Pregnancy & Child Birth

Authored by

Dr Vandana Jodhani

Website: www.authorvine.com
Email: contact@authorvine.com

First Published by Author Vine 2020
Copyright © Dr Vandana Jodhani
All Rights Reserved.

Title: Garbh Sanskara
Price: ₹ 350 | $ 7.99
ISBN: 978-81-944894-8-1

Part I

INTRODUCTION

Sanskrit word garbh means fetus,sanskar means to educate the mind in the womb.

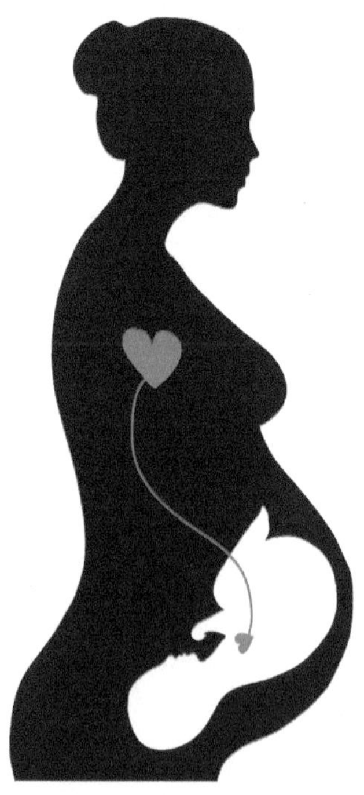

It's truly said pregnancy should be by choice, not by chance.

But if have it by chance then also you should have wonderful way to enjoy it thoroughly.

Mythological stories

Indian mythology has wonderful stories that reflect the power of garbh sanskar.

The most famous and well-known story of Abhimanyu from Mahabharata.

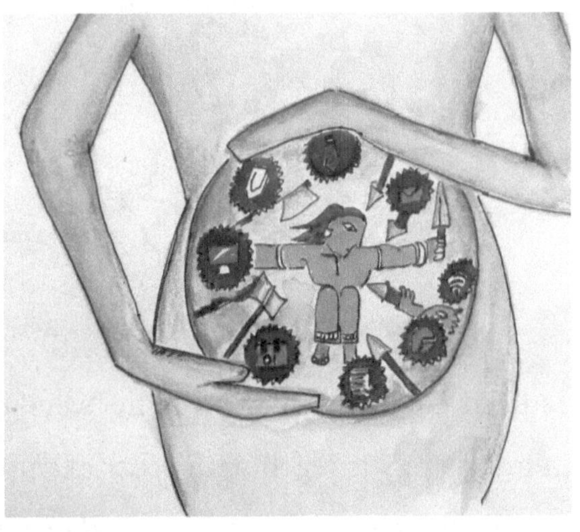

When arjun's wife was pregnant with their son, Abhimanyu. He told her about how to penetrate the chakravyue a particular war formation.when Abhimanyu become a young,he remembered his father's story. He was able to follow strategy that he had heard from his father.

Story of Prahalad

Prahalad was born into family of demons. his mother used to listen to devotional prayers, and stories about Lord Vishnu while he was in her womb. As a result he became a great devotee of Lord Vishnu. He followed well his value.

This led him to downfall of his father's evil empire

Indian mythology is reach with other examples also.

Story of lord hanuman, story of *asthavakra* great examples of that.

Garbh Sanskar is communication with unborn:

Fetus inside the mother womb can feel mothers feeling during pregnancy.

Child's personality begins to take shape inside mother's womb and it can be easily influenced by mother's mental state during pregnancy.

Scientific shreds of evidence prove that baby inside mother womb responds outside stimulation and has great ability to listen.

Having a little wonder inside womb is really GREAT feeling but at the same time, it generates lots of anxiety as well as insecurity......

TABLE OF CONTENTS

PART - II

WHAT IS NEED?

In presence world adopting advance technology, we all are dreaming high and try to achieve it at cost of individual calibre.

Along with this advance help, we are becoming more paralyzed with our self.

It generates lots of stress in our daily life.

It creates uncertain conflict at human perception level.

It hijacks the central nervous system at the preceptory level, and play very silent game along with other systems of human body.

Let's understand it ......

First of all I will discuss about certain diseases and their prevalence data......

Disease prevalence:

Psychological disorders are more common to children

Like ADHD (attention deficient hyperactive disorder),

LD (learning disorder), Irrational fear, phobias, abnormal cravings for junk food, Poor concentration in study, mood disorder, anxiety disorder, depression etc

Psychosomatic disorders are more common also like irritable bowel syndrome, hyperacidity, migraine, ulcers, conversion disorders, etc.

Hormonal disorder

Obesity, poor growth, diabetes milieus type 1, polycystic ovarian syndrome, thyroid disorder, gynecomastia etc.

In this era, These diseases are becoming common in children age group.

Comparatively, past two decades these are increasing worldwide.

Apart from that

Children's are more suffering from eczema, childhood asthma, different food allergies, upper respiratory tract infection, etc....

In this era antibiotics, anti-allergens, steroids, immunosuppressants, different pain killer, nutritional supplements are the most selling drugs in pharma industries.

In evolutionary graph human is most advance species in all living creature, then what is wrong with our system that we are suffering these disease although we have completely developed intellectual faculties in terms of evolution....

Pregnancy is a stage in a female's life.

It is natural immunosuppressive phenomena, means naturally immune system of female body becomes compromised for birth of next generation.

So, it is some total of COMPROMISE......

In this stage mental state of mother plays very crucial role for child's development.

If mother has different kind of stresses like anger, fear, anxiety, any loss(financial loss, loss of loved one, history of previous abortion, relationship break up), worry, hatred, sadness, depression etc. , these negative emotion act through psychoneuro endocrine axis in human central nervous system, and changed body's biology

Don't forget PREGNANCY IS one part of human BIOLOGY

So, it matters a lot to maintain mental health during pregnancy, otherwise it becomes PERMENANT BLUE PRINT of health of her child...

PNE Axis:

Fight or Flight Response

When we receive anything from our five senses, this information perceives through our brain.

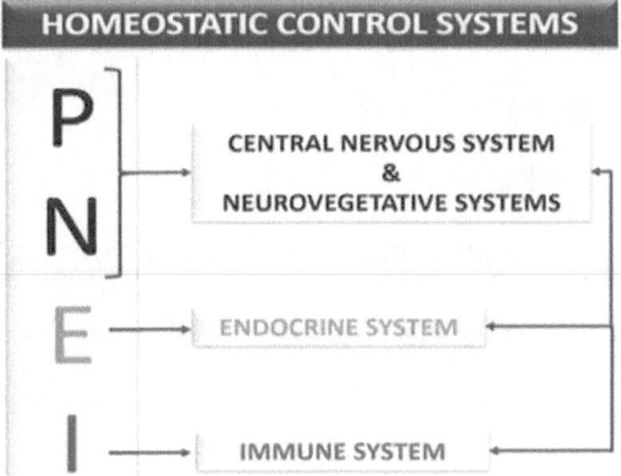

When anything perceives as a danger to human nervous system, it receives by amygdala (small almond shaped gland in the brain)

It perceives as DANGER through neurotransmitters and it stimulates pituitary gland in human nervous system.

It further stimulates adrenal gland (stress gland which located just above kidney), its secrets stress hormones in the blood circulation.

Secretion of stress hormone is one part of human biology.

In this way, there is constant, multiway and multilevel communication between mind and body.

Normally it is known as FIGHT OR FLIGHT response of human body.

It is natural defensive phenomenon of defense system.

But if there is real fear, then it is beneficial, otherwise it becomes CURS for human body.

Let's understand how......

Real fear like

Natural disasters (earthquake, tsunami....)

Facing any wild animal like tiger, snake...

Attack by someone like robbers, terrorist, or any violence

These are the real fear, in this situation FIGHT OR FLIGHT response of human body if a natural defensive mechanism.

Secretion of stress hormones, increase blood glucose

level in human body to provide energy to each and every cell.

Stress hormones increase blood pressure and narrow all the blood vessels of human body to increase blood circulation in body to provide enough oxygen as well as others macro and micronutrients to each and every cell, especially brain, because brain consume 20% more oxygen and 25% more glucose than any other part of body.

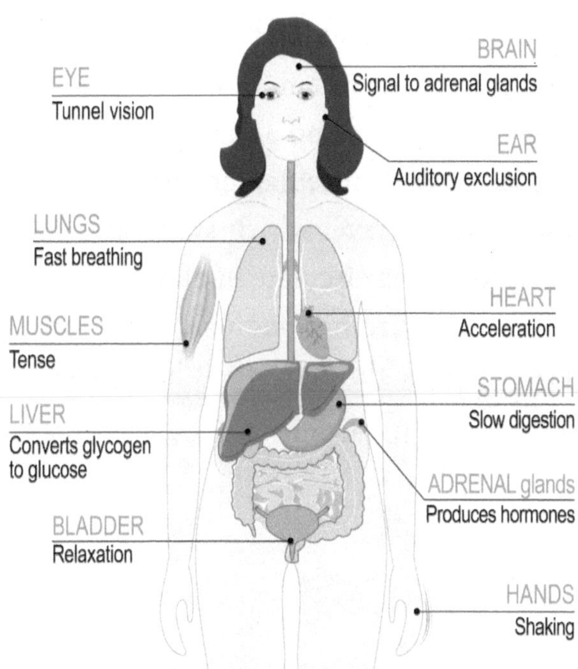

So, FIGHT AND FLIGHT response is wonderful mechanism for survivance for human body, because in real fear situation person either fight or flight, so it consumes energy and it will automatically stabilize

blood sugar and other biology.......

BUT..........................

Today neuroscientists prove that same quantity of stress hormones secrets when person feels any negative emotions like imaginary fear, anger, jealousy, sadness, aggression, worry etc....

Any negative emotion stimulates PNE axis of human body and secrets same stress hormones in the body.

Means FIGHT OR FLIGHT response of body, now after feeling of negative emotion NOBODY will going to fight or flight, means no action at physical level like to run or use your muscular power to fight....... So, high blood glucose level which stimulates though this response keeps going circulate in human body and cycle goes on....... apart from it circulate other toxins as well which are stimulate through stress hormones.

So, in this way it becomes CURS as well.

Human Perception: Real World

As I have described in earlier chapter that what we receive through our five senses it perceives by human brain.

But here I want to add some more information in terms of knowledge....

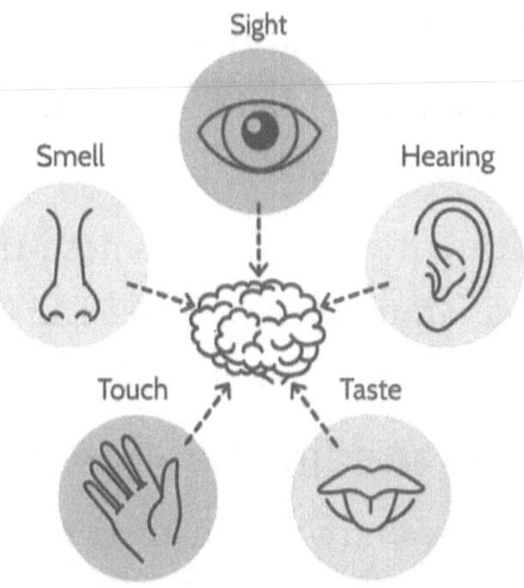

When we receive anything through our five sense, brain automatically either delete, distorted or generalized that sensory information BEFORE it perceives it.

So, delete, distortion or generalization are natural filters in human nervous system.

In other terms u you can say game changer to hijack your nervous system.

Don't forget dear friends, what we PERCIVE that becomes our REALITY.

So, in this way natural filter of human nervous system is automatically become game changer of our inner REALITY..... as well

Now, what we perceive it becomes MENTAL STATE of that particular moment. This STATE can be short lasting or long lasting. again, it defines person to person.

Mental state can be positive or negative

you can say resourceful or unresourceful

when u sense something with your five senses and its generate positive emotion like unconditional love, forgiveness, sympathy, empathy, gratitude, compassion, self-worthiness, joy, laughing, happiness etc........ then your mental state is positive or resourceful.

When you sense something through your five sense, and it generates negative feeling like anger, fear, hate, anxiety, superiority complex, inferiority complex, worry, sadness, grief, depression, guilt, jealousy, etc.......then your mental state is negative or unresourceful. Whatever your mental state is either positive or negative, you will definitely take action either verbally or nonverbally.

Verbally you can speak and express yourself through speaking.

While non verbally you will not use your word or you don't speak anything but your body language will change for that particular moment.

So, in this way you will defiantly take action.

But don't forget dear friends

'EVERY ACTION HAS A DEFINATE RE-ACTION'

The law of action-reaction (Newton's third law) explains the nature of the forces between the two interacting objects.

Sir Isaac Newton published in 1687 what is known as Newton's laws of motion, which were three physicals laws describing the relationship between the forces acting on a body and the motion of that body due to those forces.

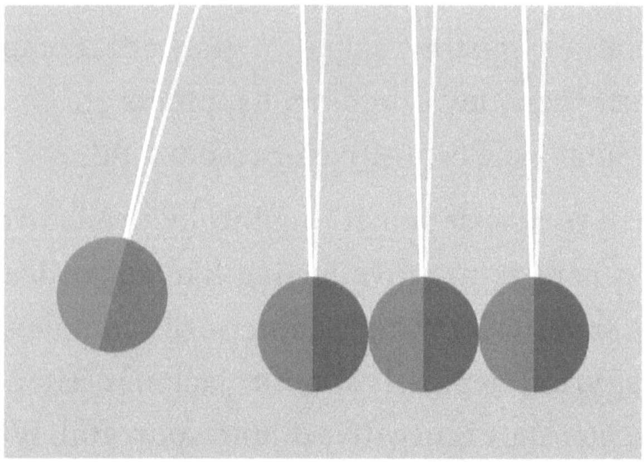

These laws of classical mechanics are still valid for the size of objects found in everyday life, such as those Newton had observed, although the description of objects outside that range (sub-atomic particles, superconducting, light speed, black holes, etc.) require more sophisticated mathematics such as those used in general relativity and quantum field theory.

Nevertheless, analogies at the macro level of mechanical physics fit Biblical principles just fine, because those types of everyday-life-objects were what Jesus used as examples when talking to the people.

He explains it at spiritual level as a **KARMA**

KARMA:

This is a term often applied to a great universal neutralizing force that eventually compensates for everything.

If a person does bad things, they will eventually reap the consequences. If a person does good things, they will eventually be rewarded in some way.

Karma is like a universal law of cause and effect -- you reap what you sow; you get what you earn; you are what you eat.

Karma might be related to the consequences of the outcome from a battle between the action and equal and opposite reaction....

GENETIC BLUE PRINT

Human body is made up of more than 60 trillion cells, so body is colony of all cells together.

They always function in form of unity, and try to maintain internal homoeostasis along with external stimulation. each cell is programmed for only health.

One individual cell does all the function which entire body can do, like respiration, circulation, excretory function, reproduction, sense like five senses.

Each cell has a potential to sense its external environment, it gets the signal and alters the activity of the gene.

Epigenetics is study of 'above' gene.

Epigenetics is the study of cellular and physiological traits, or the external and environmental factors, that turn our genes activate or deactivate.

Cell has three parts

Nucleus, cytoplasm and cell membrane.

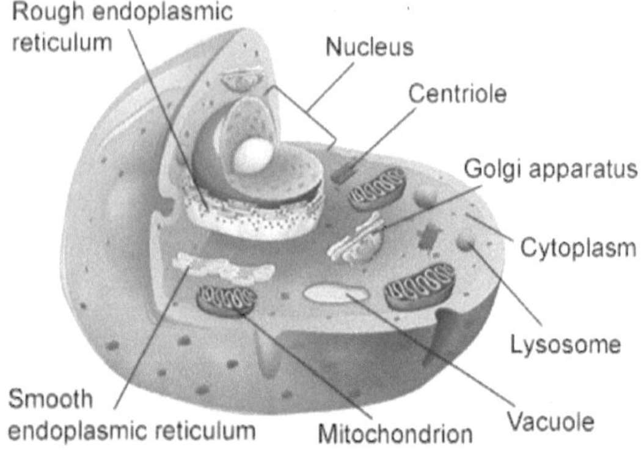

Cell membrane- the word membrane itself suggest mem BRAIN......

Cell membrane has a potential to sense the senses and able to change the behavior of its function to regulate the homoeostasis that is internal equilibrium.

One consciousness is running through entire system,

Pregnancy is a best period to give this wonderful gift of consciousness of programmed health to next generation, because one fetus is not only connected with mother cells with placenta but with one consciousness too

Fetus is combination of two parent cells which united for oneness.

During pregnancy fetus each system of the body a line with mother's physiology.

In utero fetus is dependent on parent body's system.

So, in this way it directly influenced by mother's external environment and its changes.

This wonderful journey of nine months decides about blueprints of next generation.

Pregnancy is a natural phenomenon by nature but genetic blueprint decided on bases of how much influenced by external environment.......

Epigenetic is branch of study between nonphysical dimension to physical dimension.

When DNA was discovered, might be at that time there was limitation of available technology, as well as pattern of study to entire structure of DNA is incomplete....so it was common belief that once genes patterned by two parent cell, it is for life long and permanent.

But now science has proved that human DNA can be influenced by many things.

So, epigenetics is the study of how DNA is expressed by switching genes "on" and "off" as directed by our environment. We humans have an environment which is diverse: diet, atmosphere, stress levels, fear, music, love, microbiome, belief system, prayer, and faith.

All these elements of our environment have the capability of switching our genetic switches "on" and "off."

PREGNANCY AS NATURAL PROCESS

As I describe you earlier that pregnancy is a natural process and it is one stage of life.

One female body passes through aging cycle, there are different stages

    a. Puberty - presence of menstrual cycle.

    b. Marriage - sexually activeness.

    c. **Pregnancy** - birth of next generation.

    d. Menopause - cessation or absence of menses.

These are the natural process of female body.

All females are gifted with wonderful reproductive system.

Reproductive system is made of uterus, fallopian tube, and ovaries.

Reproductive system is for reproduction of next generation means it represents CREATION....

Entire system represents felinity-one polarity in unity

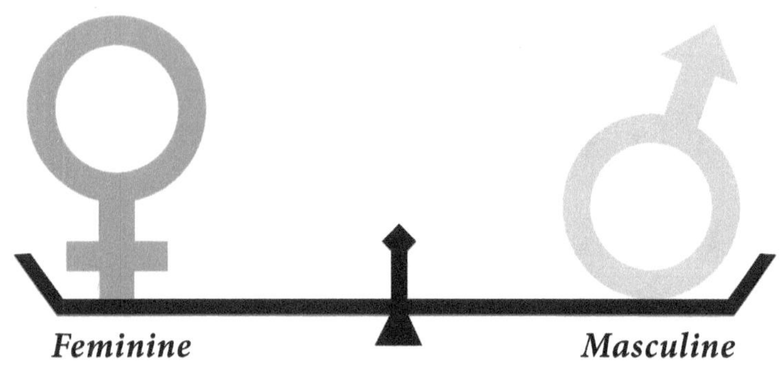

(for example, there are two sides in balance scale)

Feminine and masculine scale – female reproductive system represents feminity.

So, some total it represents FEMINITY and CREATIVITY.

Everything exists in duality in this universe. There is male in every female and female in every male.

According to medical science you can say oestrogen and progesterone hormones

Female reproductive system has predominance of female hormones, and low amount of male hormones.

As well as in male body there is predominance of male hormone and low amount of female hormones.

Once any female goes against her felinity, it indirectly stimulates her masculinity.

Because nature always tries to maintain balance.

Don't forget each cell of human body is programmed for only HEALTH

So, the body tries to maintain internal equilibrium that is homoeostasis.

In this way it stimulates to secret masculine scale of hormone inside body through auto regulatory systems, that usually medical science labbled as a hormonal imbalance

Clinically hormonal imbalance is right term because there is increased secretion of testosterone, androgen, progesterone that usually in low amount of female body.

But this is just superficial observation testing by blood sample of one female body, but there are lots of biological processes have been done at cellular level.

Each cell has its own nervous system that regulates its activity, you can say brain of the cell, each and every cell has an auto intelligence.

It has a same consciousness of rejection of her own femininity and it has positive intention to increase male hormones in female body,

Anyhow cells always support your wish to be......

So, here we cannot use term HORMONAL IMBALANCE

because body never LIE......

So, let's have a look at how female reject her own faminity

Retrospective psychological study was done on female who have diseases of reproductive system,like poly cystic ovarian diseases, infertility, fibroid uterus, cervical erosion, complications in pregnancy, endometriosis etc

they have found there is definitely rejection of her own femininity:

- Like dirty feeling about own menses
- Not liking her own appearance or look (low self-esteem about herself)
- Don't want female child as per social pressure
- Rejection of other females around her
- So, how does its effect?

Human mind is operated through more than 90% of subconscious neuron. Human subconscious brain doesn't make any different between reality and imagination. It doesn't have any LOGIC

So, entire human body operated through this more than 90% of ill logical subconscious neurons with auto regulatory system.it also regulate the chain of perception- mental state (positive/negative) -thinking-feeling- action.

So, feeling of rejection become one programme for cell, n function goes on accordingly…...

So, pregnancy is period to INTROSPECTION about self.

Any mother is part of natural process for birth of next generation which is decided by NATURE only…...

No need to take anything GRANTED, accept this wonderful process, take entire RESPONSIBILITY, and just be with it…….

Responsible Female / Mother

What is responsibility?

Responsibility is a state of having duty to deal with something or having control over something.

So, how to be responsible mother?

Each and every person born an brought up in a different environment. So, we all are different from each other.

Our individuality plays very important role in how to be responsible. Because everyone has a different definition of responsibility.

But UNIVERSAL LAW of responsibility states that

It is ability to respond appropriately to any situation.

We must take note of how we take care and look after ourselves, our children, our home, garden and pets, our possessions, our friends and family, and all of our life choices. We have a responsibility to care for ALL in our lives.

Universal Law of Responsibility tells us that true responsibility is the ability to respond to our own needs as well as to the needs of all around us such as other humans, trees, plants, whatever – ALL upon the planet.

An evolved being responds graciously to all living creatures in the Universe.

When we understand this Law of Responsibility, we no longer lay blame on anyone else or project our judgements and feeling on others.

So, automatically we speak and act from place of honesty, we take responsibility of our self and in doing.

In this way we release our self as well as others.

You only satisfied this law WHEN you have the ability to respond to that need without having an agenda, nothing to gain or lose.

When you do something for yourself or someone and it generates feeling of taking granted things then you are against of this natural phenomenon.

Stop Counting

Because there is

No PROFIT & No LOSS.

Majority of person taking responsibility to feel as a burden.

But in real sense taking responsibility takes you to door of freedom, because you don't have any account of any profit or loss in real sense.......

Taking responsibility during pregnancy indirectly make learn to baby inside mother womb, how to take responsibility. Because same consciousness runs at cellular level what mother thinks, feels, or acts during pregnancy.

For this purpose, do at least three tasks of taking responsibility every day during pregnancy.

Introspection: How to Do This?

Introspection is examining of self.

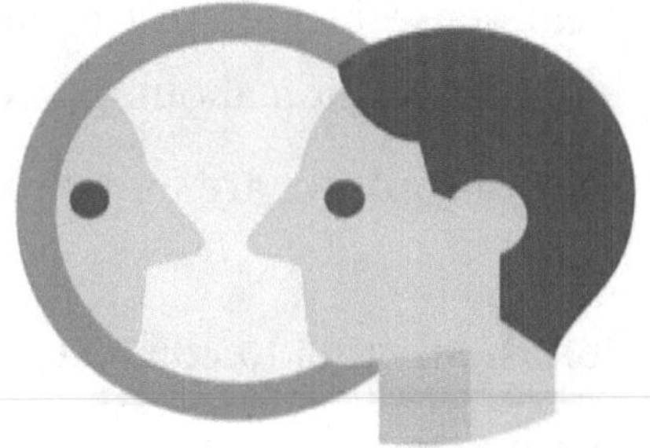

Observation of own mental state.

As I described earlier that what we perceive through our five senses it becomes MENTAL STATE

In reality we are living only one moment that is present STATE

We cannot go into past or future, even past moment passed through present and future moment will come in form of present

So, being in present moment is vital part to introspect ourselves.

Human brain is gifted with pre-frontal cortex (FRONT PART OF BRAIN) in central nervous system.

Its located frontal lobe.it is responsible for all complex behavior.

It is one of the last brain structures to develop in course of evaluation.

So, in evolutionary process humans are gifted with this developed faculties in central nervous system among all other living creatures.

We have great sense of memory of past as well as fantastic sense of imagination about future.

So, along with this gift we are forget to how to be in a present moment.

Introspection is only tool to connect our inner self

It defines with our subjective reality.it is entirely subjective phenomena.

Once you start observing your mental state in moment to moment, automatically there is stimulation of task positive network (TPN) and the activates default mode of network (DMN) in side human nervous system.

Default mode of network is operated PNE axis of

human nervous system.

So automatically it regulates by task positive network by stimulating it.

It controls stress hormones in body, can enhance biological function of the cell at the molecular level

This is one benefit at physical level, apart from that there are lots of benefits of introspection at psychological level.

Introspection can be a great source of personal knowledge-this process provides knowledge that is not possible in any other way.

Introspection connect you your higher self.

It helps you to be wise and mature, reduce your anxiety.

It connects individuals with different experience and responses, that can only be identified with this task.

WHY - PREGNANCY?

Reading this title, you might feel what a strange question?

You might get surprised but it is very important question to make you aware about this statement.

Let's understand......

Human brain has a well-developed intellectual faculty among all living creature in this world.

Humans developed fabulous technology in this world with use of this unique power, no other living creatures have done this way.

Along with this unique power and advanced technology, human brain only can understand about self and universe around us less then2 percentage with the help of science.

We can have lots of information about pregnancy, all the development stages, child birth, parenting and all about it......but why is so......science is still struggling with this STRANGE question about existence WHY?

All living creature has a same process of pregnancy without any efforts, then why so many people have a lot of struggle for this natural phenomenon.

You might have heard around you that people have to use other means like IUI, IVF (test tube baby), surrogacies.

Another living creature is doing same process in this world like eating, drinking, sleeping, reproducing without any efforts, then why humans struggling with this natural process.

So, our existence is fundamental question to us in till date.

Everything happens for a purpose, whatever it is....

Pregnancy is a part of that. Entire universe is governing with one supreme energy. It always maintains HARMONY with everything.

It expresses in dualities like

Above and Below

Before and After,

Light and Dark

Male and Female

Birth and Death.

So, two opposites to maintain universal balance, that is reality of everything.

So, each and every birth has a unique PURPOSE for existent. It has some and some meaning at deepest level.

Pregnancy should be conscious process for anyone. Because we are gifted with higher intellectual faculties by nature. Human Consciousness has very important part to deal with any things.

Consciousness and Pregnancy:

Human central nervous system is made up of more than 100 billion of neurons.

All neurons are distributed to all senses. Means human eye has neuron that perceives vision, human ear has a neuron that perceives sound, skin perceive touch, tongue perceives   taste, and nose perceive smell.

All senses weather it picture, sound, touch, smell, taste turns in to electrical signal in side nervous system. It stores in form of memory. Memory stores in form of 0,1 bite as in computer.

These neurons operated through two different minds.

Only 10% or less than of entire neuron has operated by conscious mind.

more than 90% operated by unconscious or subconscious mind

in medical term unconsciousness describe as a coma, so scientists called it subconscious mind.

Less percentage of neuron operated by conscious mind, it gifted with LOGIC

Subconscious mind doesn't have any logic.

So, our logical brain operated by less percentage of total neurons, and ill logical brain operated through more than 90% of total neurons, that is really very big amount.

Logical mind has less function in compare to ill logical mind but it is very important part of survival purpose.

Conscious mind controls short term memory, analysis, and logical aptitude

While subconscious mind controls long term memory, dreams, all kinds of desires like appetite, thirst, sex, or achieve any goal in life, emotions (positive and negative), body language, all function of body like growing nails and hair by time to time, regenerating skin, digestion of food, menstrual cycle, pregnancy, forming stool, urine, perspiration…entire body's biology autoregulate by our subconscious mind.

It programmed in such a way that it functioning day by day regularly without any command.

In sleeping stage our consciousness is down but our subconscious state working 24/7 without rest.

You have noticed that when you wake up from sleep your heart is beating, you are breathing, entire body's function is regularly going on…. So, what makes it function in a constant way in multiple way.

More than 90 percentage of entire neuron operates body at autopilot mode.

You don't have to remind your menses date, it comes by self, u don't have to remind birth of child, it does by its time duration.

Our consciousness has a LOGIC

Consciousness is what? you are aware about time, place, and about self.

Subconscious is what? When u imagine your favorite food and your mouth gets watering.it means there is no real food Infront of you but when you imagine it your subconscious neuron has a power to create its image and spontaneously it stimulates salivary gland in mouth.

So, these neurons control all the biology of human body.

Consciousness is a form of energy that existed primarily within the spiritual world and was the animating force for material life.

Physicality does not exist without the presence of consciousness.

The study of Metaphysics became focused primarily on human consciousness and its role in both the Spiritual and the Material worlds.

It also involved the study of the possibility of the existence of non-physical (spiritual) planes possessing other evolutionary realms of life besides that of the physical plan.

the study and practice of how the individual could learn to actively participate in these other, non-material, planes of existence.

Consciously attending pregnancy during nine months is very important task to shape wonderful personality of child inside mother womb.

Nonphysical Dimension to Physical Dimension.

Above title will describe journey from nonphysical dimension that is mind to physical dimension that is body

All physicality is known as matter. Matter is what we can see, feel, has certain weight or mass.

Matter is made up of basic five elements. Water, fire, air, space, earth.

Every atom in this universe is made up of these five matters.

Human body is also made up of these five constitutes,

Human body has 75% water, 12 % earth 6% air, 4% fire, rest all are ether

Space (ether)

Human breathing system represents air component, human kidney and excretory system represents water component, human bones and skeleton made up of minerals so it represents earth, human digestive system has acid that represent fire component. Human nervous is maintain balance so, it represents space or ether.

Here, I will give you one example of water.

Water is liquid by nature, when it cools at 0-degree temperature it becomes ice means it change its state that is solid. When it heats at 100-degree temperature it boils and becomes vapor. Again, it changes it state that is air.

Same atom but on patterns of arrangement it define with different name according to science.

Science explore water at the level of it constitute, function, arrangement of molecules etc. two molecules of hydrogen gas and one molecule of oxygen becomes water (H2O).

BUT……what is the previous state? what we cannot see through our eyes? or not perceive by our senses…. Nobody knows….

How it was formed on this planet first time, why it is substitute for a life?

Same way life forms from nonphysical dimension to physical dimension.

Here there are lots of role of physics, chemistry to understand this material phenomena. But I want to throw some light on metaphysics (beyond physics)

Metaphysics is the study of the true nature of reality and includes philosophy as well as physics. Both scientists and philosophers use the term "Theory of Everything" to name their carefully thought out attempts to describe the metaphysical truth of reality.

In human body we have mind and body, I am not talking about brain, because brain itself organic structure that comes under part of body.

In dead body if we dissect, we can find brain inside it but not MIND.

So, our thoughts and feelings are part of our mind.

Thoughts are nonphysical entity, no physical location in side body, but we can feel it completely.

Thought is form of energy, it converts in to electrical signal, signal travels by tiny protein like structure that is neuropeptide and connect to other synapse of neurons at micro level.

Signal creates pathways and network goes on. This is how psychneuroendocrine axis forms from nonphysical to physical dimension of human body.

So, mind and body are parts of the same system.

During pregnancy same connection form with the mother and child, because same consciousness run entire body.

So, take care of your thinking, feelings, emotions, as well as actions.

MEMORY OF WATER

Water is wonderful liquid computer.

It holds information so far.

Dr. Masaru Emoto, the Japanese scientist who is one of the most important water researchers in the world.

He studied the scientific evidence of how the molecular structure in water transforms when it is exposed to human words, thoughts, sounds and intentions.

The extraordinary life work of Dr. Emoto is documented in the New York Times Bestseller, The Hidden Messages in Water. In his book, Dr. Emoto demonstrates how water exposed to loving, benevolent, and compassionate human intention results in aesthetically pleasing physical molecular formations in the water while water exposed to fearful and discordant human intentions results in disconnected, disfigured, and "unpleasant" physical molecular formations. He did this through Magnetic Resonance Analysis technology and high-speed photographs.

If human thoughts and intention can change molecular structure of out sided water then don't forget Human body is made up of more than 75% water.

Thought is a form of energy; it has definite frequency. Frequency radiates along with its wave length. Different thoughts have different frequency that we will come to know in next chapter.

Water is mysterious liquid, this is only liquid on this planet that found in all forms like solid, liquid, and gas

Water is very good solvent; it dissolves all the minerals and important macro as well as micro nutrient.

It is wonderful transporter in human body. Water plays vital role to maintain internal body temperature according to external environment.

Apart from that water is good conductor of electricity.

During pregnancy foetus is floated in side water bag in mother's womb.

Emotional state of mother has magnificent power to stimulate molecular activity of water in side womb.

Pregnancy is the best period to be increase frequency of positive vibration, because one mother can only have nine months in her hand to use this potential along with her baby inside her womb.

Always drink water by holding positive thoughts in your mind.

Always have sense of gratitude that we are blesses with water that make us healthy forever.

Frequency and Vibrations

According to Einstein, "Everything in life is vibration."

Nikola Tesla said, "If you want to find the secrets of the universe, think in terms of energy, frequency and vibration."

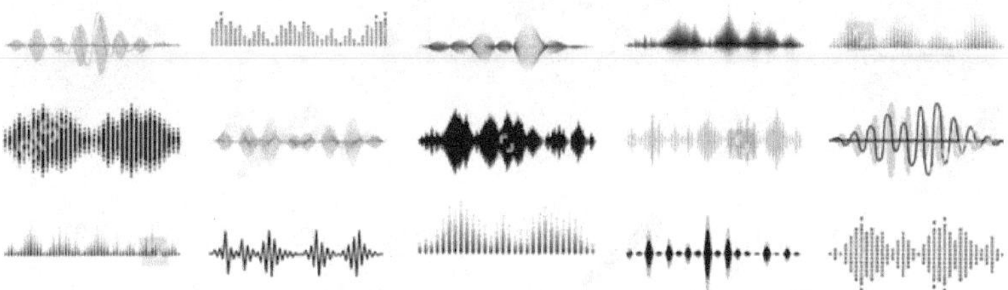

Vibration is a periodic back-and-forth motion of the particles of an elastic body or medium.

Frequency means how often…

So, in physics, some total frequency and vibration describe as a periodic back and forth motion of waves or particles per second.

It is belief that entire universe is created from one sound.

Sound is again frequency and vibration. Each sound has a different frequency and vibration according to its wave length.

Here I will discuss about MANTRAS

All MANTRAS are nothing but different form of sound.

When someone pronounces any MANTRA, it produces certain range of frequency and vibration around.

When we utter a single word from mouth while speaking it has a specific frequency and vibration that you can feel entire in your body. It has a definite action on each and every cells of our body.

Sound is such a fundamental part of our lives that we cannot escape the fact that it most definitely affects our consciousness in many ways and at many different levels.

In fact, sound has the incredible ability to induce healing and profound shifts in consciousness when applied in a very specific manner that resonates with various levels of the human body and mind.

Child in mother womb, very sensitive to sound among other senses. Child has great ability to listen inside mother womb, so pregnancy is important time to catch to teach or heal your child along with sound in side womb.

Pregnancy is actually GOLDEN period for that purpose, if one can realize its value

let's understand it scientifically

When we speak something, our entire neuron of central nervous system is started relating it.

When we repeatedly use some words with tonality, it becomes subconscious audio print for programming.

Each and every cells of human body with different system is behave nothing but subconscious programming.

So, in ancient era advice has to be given to pregnant

mother to regularly chant auspicious MANTRAS.

Because regularly chanting mantras create specific field of vibratory resonance along with different metaphors given in specific mantras, so human neuron easily get related to that specific sound and immediately started programming accordingly whatever you chant.

This science is not limited to only chanting mantras, but it has defiantly relation to each and every sound whatever mother listen during pregnancy.

So, beware of each and every word what you utter during pregnancy. Not only rhythmic sound like chanting mantras and music but the sentence you speak, the sentence you heard from someone, or you read from somewhere, it going to be audio script for your system as well as the baby inside the womb.

That's why it calls as a CONCIOUS pregnancy.

METAPHORS

A word metaphor is a noun

Metaphors means a figure of speech in which a word or phrase denoting one kind of object or action is used in place of another to suggest a likeness or analogy between them.

Human perceptions create entire INTERNAL WORLD for so and so person.

My perceptions make my internal world and your perceptions make your internal world.

It always been limited to that person, but it has a vital role to change our entire internal world anytime, anywhere, with anyone...........

In evolutionary process humans are gifted with nature's different clue to always live life in a better way.

It always available in nature, around us, as a part of

solutions.

You can also term it doctrine of nature or analogy.

The doctrine of signatures was an important aspect of folk medicine from the Middle Ages until the early modern period. Often associated with the work of herbalists and, health practitioners.

it drew upon the belief that natural objects that looked like a part of the body could cure diseases that would arise there.

Ancient healers in Christian and Muslim countries claimed that God, or Allah, deliberately made plants resemble the parts of the body they could cure.

For example, eyebright, a plant whose flower looks like bright blue eyes, was used to treat eye diseases. The use of eyebright for this purpose was still common in the 1700s.

Today the idea of 'like cures like' lies at the heart of modernscience of homeopathy.

But metaphors have some different meaning then analogy.

Metaphor is a shape of the word or sentence that is very sufficient to create image or figure inside human brain.

Metaphor is very powerful tool to use human nervous system, to create our life whatever we want.

Human subconsciousness doesn't have any logic.

Human subconscious PROGRAMMING has typical coding pattern.

It cannot understand any language. Here memory stores in form of vision, sound, touch, smell or taste.

It means whatever we perceive through our five senses that recorded by 90% of human subconscious neuron which is store of unlimited memory.

Vision, sound, touch, smell and taste are the vital component of that deep-rooted memory.

Metaphor has power to create good image to human subconscious programming.

For example

He is walking like a lion.

Here lion is metaphor to walking style, that indirectly reflect confidante and fearless walk......

Unique and standing out of the crowd.

We knowingly and unknowingly give lots of metaphor to our brain in day to day life.

It can be positive as well as negative, it depends how you use it.

Regular chanting mantras give positive and strong metaphor to human subconsciousness to program healthy and successful life.

During pregnancy, one mother must give strong and healthy metaphors to shape child's personality in mother's womb.

POWER OF WORDS

Human being is gifted with speech among other living animals.

It is very powerful tool to express self as well as to communicating with others.

During pregnancy unborn child is very closed to his/her mother's voice. child in mother's womb easily recognize mother's voice first.

Here I will explain about two kind of voice.

External voice- which we speak to others/listen by others

Internal voice- which running at mental script after feeling something.

Words are the powerful force that can construct as well as destruct according to use of it.

we must focus on the conversation with awareness

and definite purpose.

During the conversation, we must listen patiently, speak gently, and tell the truth as we understand it.

one must align our words, voice inflection and tone, eye expression, body language, and actions with our inner awareness in an honest exchange.

Words are not simply sounds caused by air passing through our larynx. Words have real power.

Words do more than convey information.

Words can wound or can heal anyone. The power to use words is a unique and powerful gift from the God.

Words are enough capable to generate emotion and can instantly change state of mind.

Use powerful and positive words, that can generate positive energy and positive emotions inside you, that can instantly radiate through billions of neuronal pathways to your child inside the womb.

Words are the vehicle for change and inspiration.

Words turn dreams and visions into reality, they

give life to all that remains hidden and kept away.

words allow ideas, innovations and movements to see the light of day when in any other circumstance.

Spoken words to others as well as listen from others, source doesn't matter but human's vast numbers of neurons get related to it, and generate so and so feelings, instantly started multiway communication with entire body by neural pathways and capacity to change physiology of human body.

Always use words wisely and consciously, because not only affect one person but all who receive it and relate it has a same action which I have described.

Research suggests that rhyme words or rhythm in sentences easy way to learn in early age group, because that is sufficient to create emotions so it helps to increase awareness.

Breathing and Consciousness During Pregnancy

Breathing is not only inhaling and exhaling the air, breathing is vital process that connects self as well as to baby in side womb.

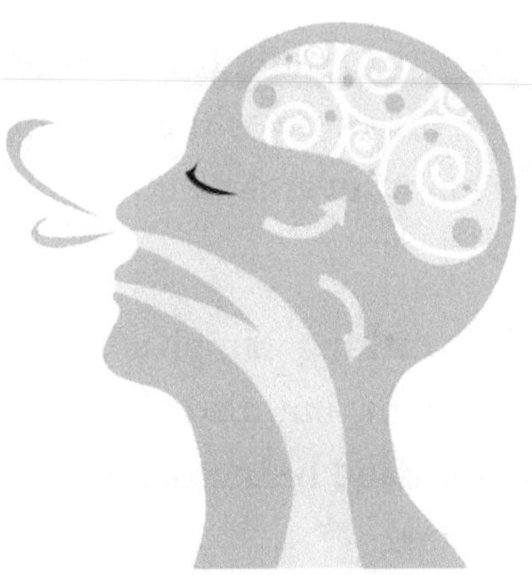

Breathing is only tool to make person aware about PRESENT.

Billions of neurons in side human body instantly get ready to change any mental state once you change breathing patterns.

Research on breathing shows that nasal breathing plays an important role in coordinating electrical brain signals in the olfactory "smell" cortex (the brain regions that directly receive input from our nose, which then coordinates the amygdala (which processes emotions) and the hippocampus (responsible for both memory and emotions).

We know that the "smell" system is closely linked to the limbic brain regions that affect emotion, memory and behaviour, which is why sometimes a particular smell or fragrance can evoke very strong emotional memories.

One way to understand this is to think of the system as an orchestra: our nasal breathing is the grand conductor, setting the tempo for the slow playing of the smell regions of the brain while weaving in the faster rhythms of the emotion and memory regions.

Conscious breathing emphasizes not only the breathing component, but also the mental component of paying attention and becoming aware of mind, body and breath together.

Conscious breathing becomes a path to insight.

Our breath is powerful enough to regulate emotions and help us gain clarity, and to fully do so we must also make the effort to center our minds to the here and now. In this way, breathing is only natural tool to connect your consciousness to baby in side womb as well as remote control of brain of mother as well as child.

Apart from it breathing has so many benefits at physical level.

Deep breath in and out give movement to diaphragm in abdomen, so there is natural massage of internal organ like kidney, liver, spleen, intestine, as well as baby inside mother womb.

Conscious breathing detoxifies lymphatic system of the body that carries different toxins.

Deep breathing stimulates endorphins that are natural pain killers.

Deep Breathing provides more oxygen to each and every cell in your body. With the supply of oxygen to the brain this increases the muscles in your body.

Oxygen travels through your bloodstream by attaching to hemoglobin in your red blood cells. This in turn then enriches your body to metabolize nutrients and vitamins.

The digestive organs such as the stomach receive more oxygen, and hence operates more efficiently. The digestion is further enhanced by the fact that the food is oxygenated more.

Deep breathing activates the parasympathetic nervous system, bringing us into a relaxed state. It functions in the opposite way to the sympathetic nervous system, which stimulates activities associated with the fight-or-flight response.

Deep breathing reduced carbon dioxide and waste metabolites, that way it improves blood circulation to entire body.

Regular breathing exercise makes person look younger and more confident.it has a marked effect on aging process.

Developmental Stages in Fetus:

MONTH	Development	Body Parts	Size
First	Egg-fertiliza-tion, sac forma-tion, Placenta devel-op	Face- large circle for eyes, mouth jaw, throat, Tiny heart, (beats 62/min at end of 4 weeks)	About ¼ inch long.

Second	The neural tube is well formed. (brain, spinal cord and other neural tissue of the CNS) Digestive tract and sensory organs begin to develop. Bone starts to replace cartilage.	Face, ear as a little fold of skin, tiny buds for arm and legs. Fingers, toes and eyes are also forming.	1 inch long and weighs about 1/30 of an ounce.
Third	Reproductive organs By the end of the third month, your baby is fully formed. All the organs and extremities are present and will continue to mature in order to become functional. The circulatory and urinary systems are working and the liver produces bile.	Baby can open and close fists and mouth. Fingernails and toenails are beginning to develop and the external ears are formed. The beginnings of teeth form	At end of third month, your baby is about 4 inches long and weighs about 1 ounce.

Fourth	Heartbeat may now be audible to medical device. The nervous system is starting to function. The reproductive organs and genitalia are now fully developed.	The fingers and toes are well-defined. Eyelids, eyebrows, eyelashes, nails, and hair are formed. Teeth and bones become denser. Your baby can even suck his or her thumb, yawn, stretch, and make faces.	By the end of the fourth month, 6 inches long and weighs about 4 ounces.

Fifth	Baby begin to move that calls Quickening.	Hair on baby's head. shoulders, back, and temples are covered by a soft fine hair called lanugo. This hair protects your baby and is usually shed at the end of the baby's first week of life. The baby's skin is covered with a whitish coating called vernix caseosa. This "cheesy" substance is thought to protect baby's skin from the long exposure to the amniotic fluid. This coating is shed just before birth.	By the end of the fifth month, your baby is about 10 inches long and weighs from 1/2 to 1 pound.

Sixth	Baby responds to sounds by moving or increasing the pulse. You may notice jerking motions if baby hiccups.	Your baby's skin is reddish in color, wrinkled, and veins are visible through the baby's translucent skin. Baby's finger and toe prints are visible. The eyelids begin to part and the eyes open.	By the end of the sixth month, about 12 inches long and weighs about 2 pounds.
Seventh	Baby's hearing is fully developed. changes position frequently and responds to stimuli, including sound, pain, and light. The amniotic fluid begins to diminish	Baby will continue to mature and develop reserves of body fat.	At the end of the seventh month, your baby is about 14 inches long and weighs from 2 to 4 pounds.

Eight	Develop reserves of body fat. brain is developing rapidly at this time, and your baby can see and hear. Most internal systems are well developed, but the lungs may still be immature.	Continue to mature	About 18 inches long and weighs as much as 5 pounds.
Nineth	The lungs are nearly fully developed. reflexes are coordinated so can blink, close the eyes, turn the head, grasp firmly, and respond to sounds, light, and touch. Baby is definitely ready to enter the world!	Continue to grow	About 18 to 20 inches long and weighs about 7 pounds.

As anyone can understand about this development, but I want to make your attention to wonderful and mysterious process that happening since century.

We all have a same journey, why is that so?

What is relationship between product of pregnancy to mother cell?

Let's understand……

Pregnancy is a result of union of two parent cells.

One parent cell unite with other one, in that union experience new state of consciousness –'orgasm'

New state of consciousness is qualitatively far superior than normal consciousness.

Two different polarities unite and become one result in 'ecstasy'. – consequently state of union.

Sexuality is one attempt to unite opposite.

United consciousness runs through each cell's consciousness of reproductive system.

Mirroring and matching.

Human Neuron has unique characteristics of mirroring and matching.

Cells are equally intelligent to produce exact replica of self, by this unique characteristic of mirror and matching.

First united parent cell is known as a zygote.

Zygote rapidly divide into two different cells according to science but meta morphologically it is copy of self…..

Two to four, four to eight, eight to sixteen……

whatever meta morphologically again copy of self......
so it tries to match the maximum possibilities at all the
levels.....

Cells function and structure also influenced by
environmental factors.

So, new life begins with all this influenced and
informative subconscious programming.

What are Emotions?

Emotions are biological states associated with the nervous system brought on by neurophysiological changes variously associated with thoughts, feelings, behavioral responses, and a degree of pleasure or displeasure.

The word emotion is plural noun that means a strong feeling deriving from one's circumstances, mood, or relationships with others.

Human has different emotions at different time.it is changeable, it may be loop cycle from one feeling to other

The limbic system is the area of the brain most heavily implicated in emotion and memory. Its structures include the hypothalamus, thalamus, amygdala, and hippocampus. The hypothalamus plays a role in the activation of the sympathetic nervous system, which is a part of any emotional reaction.

Here we will see it from different direction.

Emotions are nothing but E-motion means energy in motion.

In this entire universe nothing is still, or steady

Everything is in motion, our galaxy is spinning, entire solar system is spinning, our mother earth is spinning, we have studied in physics that at subatomic level electron is spinning in orbit.

If we think in term of natural sources of energy like water, air, fire is always in constantly flow.

Storage water gets fungus. Close place has dirty smell because of no circulation of air, so everything has its own effect on fabric of universe.

All emotions are energy, and energy can never be generated or destroy. It always means to be TRANSFORM from one state to other.

Energy has a vibrational frequency, and energy forms and transforms. Emotions move, have a vibrational frequency, take form, are changing, and impermanent. we continually change from one emotion to another,

Emotions are changeable mental state. One moment you can be happy and other you can be sad or depressed. It's always changeable. It may be short lasting or long lasting it defines person to person.

You have never felt an emotion that was permanent.

Be aware about yourself, then you will realize your true nature.

Here I will describe emotions in different parts on basis of its expressions

A) Emotions as a feeling:

Human mind is collectively model of sensory-perceptual interpretation.

Whatever human body receive through five senses; it naturally gets filter by this sensory- perceptual interpretation. Either it deletes, either distorted or generalize the perceptions.

Feelings spin off from your mind's activity. That is responsible to release of dormant bio-field energies of past emotional pain resurfacing from a trigger.

It stores in form of memory that is coding system in form of bites as usual like computer.

B) Emotions at level of behavior

Each and every emotion decide chain reaction as a behavior. It could be expressive or suppressive, in either way it transforms it's state.

Either person will react or suppress, in either way the emotional energy remains lodged in the bio-fields of the body creating tension, illness, or manifesting at inappropriate times.

Patterns of different behavior record in form of different neural pathways and behaving according to it.

C)Emotions as biology or physiology

Emotions radiate in body and express itself as biology or physiology, physical sensations are generated from physiological/ biological reaction.

It includes the release of catecholamines (hormones & neurotransmitters) in the brain.

For example, the energy physical sensation may take the form of fear, it stimulate PNE axis of central nervous system and releases stress hormones in body, where you feel your body prepares for action: breath goes in, heat rises, heart rate and blood pressure increase, pupil widely dilated, blood sugar increases, goose bombs and sweating on skin, muscle tension/contraction, trembling of hands and legs and increase frequency of stool and urine.

So, in this way emotions feel in form of physical sensation.

D) Emotions as a Energy

One individual Human cell does all the function what entire body do, like respiration, circulation, reproduction etc. in this way cell receive all senses as a sensory receiver.

As all senses are recording in form of electrical signal.

Cells have average membrane potential, that formed by intracellular and extracellular exchange

The average "membrane potential" for a cell is 70 millivolts OR .07 volts (this the electrical charge difference between the inside of the cell, separated by the cell membrane, from the charge just outside the cell membrane).

There are 50 trillion cells X .07volts = 3.5 trillion volts.

Using nano-scale voltmeters, biologist have now found that within a cell, "all of the 13 regions (of the cytoplasm) we measured had high electric field strength---as high as 15 million volts per meter"

Electrical voltages have vibration and frequency.

Emotions have voltage.

The vibrational frequencies of emotions are on a vertical dimension of contraction and expansion relative to the vibrational voltage of a particular emotion.

Emotions resonate with the vibrational frequency that they generate.

The higher the vibrational frequency, then the higher the expansion, and the greater the Life Force in your cells.

The lower the vibrational frequency, then the greater the contraction, and the lesser of Life Force in your cells.

The emotional energy vibration can be like ripples on a water, it tries to maintain rhythm.

The emotional energy vibration can be like a overwhelming and overlapping river in a state of fright.

The emotional energy vibration can be like shattered tremors such as in a state of anxiety.

The emotional energy vibration can be intensifying charged current like lightning in rain, in the state of anger.

Emotional energy can be like a tsunami wave that hits you with full force like in the state of grief pulling you down and under.

The emotional energy of depression feels very heavy as if you are almost lifeless.

So , human body is fully resonant with life force.

It may resonant with higher as well as lower frequency.

Different emotions vibrating with different frequencies.

Part II

Frequency and Vibrations

Hear I explained about some points of physics

Imagine sine wave moving at a fixed wave speed, wavelength is inversely proportional to frequency of the wave, means waves with higher frequencies have shorter wavelengths, and lower frequencies have longer wavelengths.

Any wave has two physical characteristics: amplitude and wavelength.

The amplitude of a wave is the height of a wave as measured from the highest point on the wave (peak or crest) to the lowest point on the wave. Wavelength refers to the length of a wave from one peak to the next.

Wavelength is directly related to the frequency of a given wave form.

Frequency refers to the number of waves that pass a given point in a given time period and is often expressed in terms of hertz (Hz), or cycles per second. Longer wavelengths will have lower frequencies, and shorter wavelengths will have higher frequencies.

Wavelength and frequency are inversely related so that longer waves have lower frequencies, and shorter waves have higher frequency.

Human mind is processor that continue process this frequency and vibration with help of biochemical molecules.

Biochemical which generated by any emotions is known as a feeling.

Again, vibration is the emotion that created by chemical changes resulting from previous emotion. And loop goes on.

Positive and negative emotions describe on bases of the balance of the oscillations.

Positive emotions come from balanced vibrations. Negative emotions come from imbalanced vibrations.

First of all, we will understand frequency of our sensory perceptions then will go to emotions.

Eye – Vision

Human eyes can see things only which can reflect the light.

We cannot see the light absorber things, as a visual apparatus it is out of human eyes capacity.

What we can see is known as 'The visible spectrum'– that is portion of the larger electromagnetic spectrum.

The visible spectrum in humans is associated with wavelengths that range from 380 to 740 nm—a very small distance, since a nanometer (nm) is one billionth of a meter.

In humans, light wavelength is associated with perception of color. Within the visible spectrum, our experience of red is associated with longer wavelengths, greens are intermediate, and blues and violets are shorter in wavelength.

(An easy way to remember this is the mnemonic ROYGBIV: red, orange, yellow, green, blue, indigo, violet.)

The amplitude of light waves is associated with our experience of brightness or intensity of color, with larger amplitudes appearing brighter.

Color	Wavelength interval	Frequency interval
violet	~ 430 to 380 nm	~ 700 to 790 THz
blue	~ 500 to 430 nm	~ 600 to 700 THz
cyan	~ 520 to 500 nm	~ 580 to 600 THz
green	~ 565 to 520 nm	~ 530 to 580 THz
yellow	~ 590 to 565 nm	~ 510 to 530 THz
orange	~ 625 to 590 nm	~ 480 to 510 THz
red	~ 740 to 625 nm	~ 405 to 480 THz

Ear - Hearing

The audible range of sound frequencies for human ear is between 20 and 20000 Hz, with greatest sensitivity to those frequencies that fall in the middle of this range.

Like light waves, the physical properties of sound waves are associated with various aspects of our perception of sound.

The frequency of a sound wave is associated with our perception of that sound's pitch.

High-frequency sound waves are perceived as high-pitched sounds,

while low-frequency sound waves are perceived as low-pitched sounds.

Although wave amplitude is generally associated with loudness, there is some interaction between frequency and amplitude in our perception of loudness within the audible range.

For example, a 10 Hz sound wave is inaudible no

matter the amplitude of the wave.

A 1000 Hz sound wave, on the other hand, would vary dramatically in terms of perceived loudness as the amplitude of the wave increased.

The loudness of a given sound is closely associated with the amplitude of the sound wave.

Higher amplitudes are associated with louder sounds. Loudness is measured in terms of decibels (dB), a logarithmic unit of sound intensity.

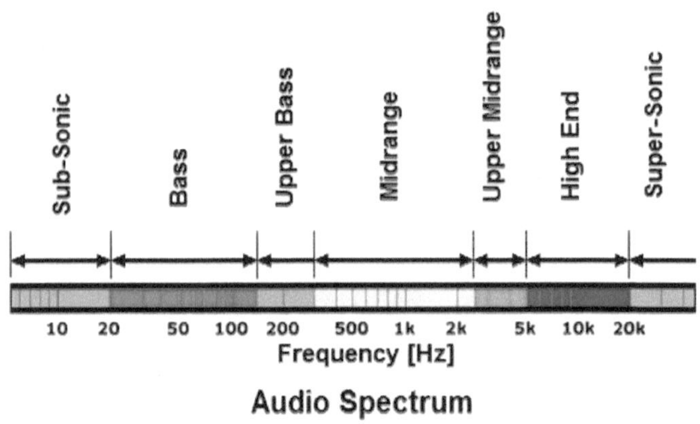

Audio Spectrum

Nose-Smell

Vibrational modes within the range of 1,400–3,500 cm−1 were responsible for the activation of olfactory receptor sites.

It was vibrations of ~700 cm−1 or less that were responsible for any activation process.

Similarly, strong band within the 150–200 cm−1 range.

Tongue-Taste

Different taste depends up on concentration of particular substance.

Skin-Touch

Skin is largest sense organ in human body.

Externally skin sense heat, cold, smooth, rough, hard, soft, pressure etc.

But internally touch describe as an all kind of subjective sensations.

For example, if you have pain any where in your body, that particular pain has different character.

It could be pulsating, bursting, stitching, squeezing, etc.

Apart from that different kind of sensation like chocking, burning, twitching, butterfly sensation etc.... all are internal touch.

So, different sensations have a different frequency.

Emotions are nothing but internal touch.

Let's understand different frequency of emotions.

As I explained earlier that Emotions resonate with the vibrational frequency that they generate.

The higher the vibrational frequency, then the

higher the expansion, and the greater the Life Force in your cells.

The lower the vibrational frequency, then the greater the contraction, and the lesser of Life Force in your cells.

Positive and negative emotions describe on bases of the balance of the oscillations.

Positive emotions come from balanced vibrations. Negative emotions come from imbalanced vibrations.

Or we can say positive emotion is balanced energy and have higher frequency. While negative emotion is imbalanced energy and have lower frequency.

Negative emotions like anger, fear, hatred, anxiety, superiority complex, inferiority complex, guilt, grief, disgusts,rage,melancholy, etc.

Collectively all negative emotion has lower frequency less than 175 Hz.

Positive emotion has higher frequency more than 200 Hz.

Let's understand positive emotions in detail, because pregnancy is golden chance to implanting all positive characteristic to unborn child inside mother womb.

So, one mother must focus on positive emotions.

Let's understand general physiology of emotion and then will discuss specific emotions.

Role of Human nervous System to Feel Emotion.

The nervous system as a whole includes the Central Nervous System, consisting of brain and spinal cord, and the Peripheral Nervous System, whose nerve fibres connect all parts of the body with the Central Nervous System.

Most of the control and organizing functions of the CNS are carried out by neurons which do all the processing and communication.

The spinal cord mainly serves to channel sensory information to the brain, and motor commands from the brain.

The limbic system (part of brain) is made up of the hippocampus which is essential for the formation of long-term memories and the amygdala which appears to be a centre of emotions (as an alarming signal of fear or danger).

It is an area of intimate interaction between hypothalamic and cortical information processing.

It plays a role in emotions, learning and autonomic regulations.

The Peripheral Nervous System, on the other hand, consists of nerves, which are bundles of individual axons of neurons.

The Peripheral Nervous System is further subdivided into two branches, the Somatic Nervous System which controls organs under voluntary control (mainly muscles) and the Autonomic Nervous System which regulates individual organ function and internal equilibrium that is homoeostasis.

The Somatic Nervous System plays an important role in emotion, since it innervates the facial and postural muscles that execute the expressive patterns of the emotions.

These patterns are highly important in the intra-organism emotion process and communication.

Autonomic nervous system controls fight and flight responses.

Neurotransmitters are chemicals made by neurons and used by them to transmit signals to the other neurons or non-neuronal cells.

the primary functional unit is a cell called the neuron. All sensations, movements, thoughts, memories, and feelings are the result of signals that pass-through neurons, which are the building blocks of the nervous system.

Neurons are the cells within our bodies that receives and transform information.

The neurotransmitters influence the activity of the brain, and they are of central importance to the pharmacological therapy of thought disorders, mood disorders, and anxiety disorders.

Dopamine, serotonin, acetylcholine, histamine, GABA and glutamate are some of the important neurotransmitters.

Hormones are chemical substances made by endocrine glands. These glands pass the hormones directly into the bloodstream, which carries them around the body, that is, hormones carry messages from glands to cells to maintain chemical levels in the bloodstream that achieve homeostasis.

EMOTIONS AND FREQUENCY

Now, lets understand different emotion and its effect on human body.

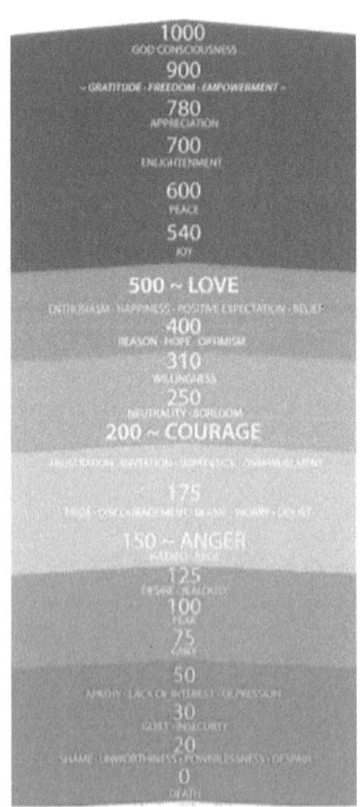

Love

528Hz frequency

If I talk about definition of love or any emotion it may define person to person. an intense feeling of deep affection.

Emotions are subjective experiences, and subjective feelings depend on individuality.

Dictionary meaning of love deep affection or

a great interest and pleasure in something.

Love is, undeniably, a nutritional need for all humans. Our physical, mental, and emotional well-being greatly depend on receiving nurturance and positive touch from healthy, reciprocal relationships.

Science of love:

love is MENTAL STATE and strong positive emotion which generate feeling of please.

Human behavior researcher, divides the experience of love into three partly overlapping stages:

Lust, Attraction, and Attachment.

Lust is the feeling of sexual desire; romantic attraction determines what partners mates find attractive and pursue, conserving time and energy by choosing;

Attachment involves sharing a home, parental duties, mutual defense, and in humans involves feelings of safety and security.

Three distinct neural circuitries, including neurotransmitters, and three behavioral patterns, are associated with these three romantic styles.

Lust is the initial passionate sexual desire that promotes sexual communicate and involves the increased release of chemicals such as testosterone and estrogen.

These effects rarely last more than a few weeks or months.

Attraction is the more individualized and romantic desire for a specific candidate for mating, which develops out of lust as commitment to an individual mate form.

people fall in love, the brain consistently releases a certain set of chemicals, including the neurotransmitter hormones, dopamine, norepinephrine, and serotonin.

Attachment link with oxytocin and vasopressin high level.

But here I want to make you notice about love at spiritual level.

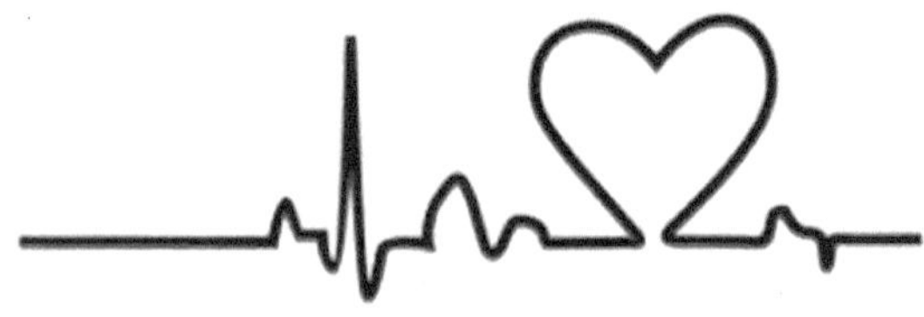

The yoga tradition describes Absolute Reality as satchidananda—meaning that it is pure beingness, present everywhere and in everything (sat), that it is innately conscious (chit), and that it is the essence of joy and love (Ananda).

The practice of love—actions and attitudes that create an atmosphere of kindness, acceptance, and unity in ourselves and in those around us.

How can we know that our self is in influence of in real sense of love that really mean to touch our spiritual dimension?

Feeling of UNITY: the moment when we unite with something or someone without any rules and regulation or we can say any condition, that realize sense of unity.

When one is ready to remove ' I' from sense of awareness and shift to 'we', that permits self to unite.

When we have sense of unity, we don't need to learn how to love others. Itself feeling of unity define attachment. Attachment automatically feel same emotions what other feels without any explanations.

So, automatically it generates sense of responsibility.

Sense of responsibility activate will, drive and motivation at mental level. And itreflects as an action and behavior of so and so person.

During pregnancy resonant yourself with 528 Hz, and take opportunity to implant same positive characteristic to unborn child.

Forgiveness

432 Hz frequency

Dictionary meaning of forgiveness

Noun: forgiveness: action or process of forgiving or being forgiven.

Psychologists generally define forgiveness as a conscious, deliberate decision to release feelings of resentment toward a person or group who has harmed you, regardless of whether they actually deserve your forgiveness.

> *"Forgiveness is giving up the wish that things could be different".*
>
> *—Valarie Harper*

Physiology of forgiveness:

According to internationally renowned cardiologist, Herbert Benson, "There's something called the physiology of forgiveness. Being unable to forgive other people's faults is harmful to one's health."

Forgiveness is about you and your health. When you forgive, you tend to benefit more than the one who is forgiven."

The discovery of 'mirror neurons' in the brain point out that what you look at and think about changes your brain—forgive for the benefits it provides and avoid ending up resentful, bitter, and sick, with perhaps a shortened life span.

Unforgiveness restore negativity towards thing or person, when it holds at subconscious level, it reflects as a form of expression and behaviour at physical level.

Let's understand how it allows to physical body.

As we know that mind and body are parts of same system.

Any mental state is entangled state of mind and body.

Unforgiveness generate bitterness and resentment that are shades of emotions of suppressed anger.

It holds as a chronic stressor in form of long-term memory. That driven as a same consciousness to each and every cellular consciousness via psycho neuroendocrine axis.

Human body vibrates same frequency what it carries at energy level.

Human thoughts and feelings generate at energy level.

As I describe you earlier emotions are nothing but ENERGY in MOTION.

Forgiveness release from bondage of self as well as others.

But FORGIVENESS is always CHOICE.

Act of forgiveness act as awareness about self, that shuttle process has very micro action on human nervous system.

Being aware about self consciously active task positive network in central nervous system, as well as it deactivates default mode of network.

Default mode of network, regulates human biology and secretion of stress hormones.

The act of forgiving allows the body to turn down the manufacture of catabolic chemicals, and instructs the subconscious to dissolve negative feelings from the mind.

If you choose decisional and emotional forgiveness, studies have shown many positive outcomes, including: Healthier relationships, Lower blood pressure , Less anxiety, stress, and hostility ,reduce symptoms of depression, Lower risk of alcohol, substance abuse compassion, kindness, and peace, mental, physical, and spiritual health

Awareness about self for forgiving self and others takes person to path of inner journey as well.

During pregnancy practice of forgiveness is generate 432hz frequency.

This frequency transform grief into joy and guilt in to forgiveness.

Practice of forgiveness connect consciousness with neural network of baby inside mother womb, that will also help to lower down of emotional burden during pregnancy.

As long as you don't forgive, who and whatever it is will occupy a rent-free space in your mind well said by Isabelle Holland.

Gratitude

963hz frequency

Dictionary meaning of gratitude is

Noun: Gratitude

The quality of being thankful; readiness to show appreciation for and to return kindness.

Gratitude is one kind of attitude. It is MENTAL STATE for present moment.

Gratitude is high frequency emotions among all positive emotions, or you can say "mother "of all emotions.

Practice of Gratitude is not only helpful for spiritual growth, it has a great role to control human biology as well.

Daily practice of gratitude stimulate positive feedback loop inside body, it also increases mental strength.

Reserch suggest that participants overwhelmingly reported strong feelings of gratitude, deep engagement in the task, and, perhaps even more importantly, an increased empathy as a result of participating in the study.

when participants reported those grateful feelings, their brains showed activity in a set of regions located in the medial pre-frontal cortex, an area in the frontal lobes of the brain where the two hemispheres meet.

This area of the brain is associated with understanding other people's perspectives, empathy, and feelings of relief.

This is also an area of the brain that is massively connected to the systems in the body and brain that regulate emotion and support the process of stress relief.

So practice of gratitude shapes human personality that can definitely improve strong relationship with surrounding people.

It stimulate that area of brain which stimulate in a same way one person get social bonding and stress relief.

Gratitude activates the hypothalamus, one of the most glamorous parts of the brain, but a seriously important one.

The hypothalamus is responsible for regulating all kinds of bodily functions, including hunger, sleep, body temperature, metabolism, and how the body grows.

It's one of the body's control centres, and gratitude seems to motivate it to excel.

When you focus the things, you have in your life that you could be grateful for: all the nurturing relationships, the material comforts, your body, and the mind that allows you to really understand yourself and everything around you.

It connects you with everything in creation, it opens field of heart to accept everything around you.

Energy flows where attention goes......

I will say gratitude is important MENTAL DIET, it is a super-duper vitamin for detox your brain.

Research suggests some physical benefit of daily practice of gratitude.

It helps to regulate sleep pattern and regulate blood pressure.

Let's have a look of research data

Current research published in Personality and Individual Differences explains that what I felt was the physical effects of gratitude. In fact, gratitude can:

- Lower your blood pressure
- Improve immune function
- Lower cortisol levels by 23%
- Improve sleep quality by 10%
- Lower blood sugar levels by 13%
- Gratitude "blocks toxic emotions, such as sadness, envy, resentment, regret and depression, anger which can destroy our happiness.

So, it is well said that It's impossible to feel regretful and grateful at the same time."

During pregnancy practice of gratitude is very crucial part of garbh sanskar.

It generates faith in self. It makes you spiritually disciplined person.

Gratitude develops humanity, and great virtue of warmth in our heart, that connect us with our source of creation.

Practice of gratitude makes our journey easy from "*I*" to "*WE*".

So, say thank you to your unborn child, because of him or her you are enjoying your motherhood.

Say thank you to nature that nature has selected you for baby angel that you carry in your womb.

Courage

852 Hz frequency

Dictionary meaning of courage:

Courage is the quality shown by someone who decides to do something difficult or dangerous, even though they may be afraid.

Noun

The attitude of facing and dealing with anything recognize as dangerous, difficult, or painful, insteadof withdrawing from it; quality of being fearless or brave.

Courage is free will to be comfortable in any uncomfortable situation.it is an attribute of positive character that makes us worthy of respect.

To understand courage first we need to understand what is fear?

Fear is negative emotion or feeling that generate through danger.

Fear perceived by amygdala in brain. By Psycho neuroendocrine axis it hijacks entire human nervous as well as human physiology.

As I mention in earlier chapter how does it effect on human body and change chemical reaction in side body.

Human body vibrates with around 19 Hz frequency under emotion of fear.

While courage involves facing our deep-seated fear of psychological instability, development of psychological courage is essential to the well-being of self.

Courage is physiological as well as psychological concept to be fearless even though experiencing high grade of fear.

Neurology and Courage:

Research has done to evaluate the neurological function in terms of courage, by making object closer and farther away.

There is high somatic arousal (assessed by skin conductance response) accompanied by low subjective fear (assessed by fear self-ratings) or high subjective fear accompanied by low somatic arousal activity in a brain region called the subgenual anterior cingulate cortex correlated positively with the level of subjective fear when choosing to act courageously but not when choosing to succumb to fear.

Further, activity in a series of temporal lobe structures was decreased when the level of fear increased and the individual chose to overcome their fear.

So, collectively subgenual anterior cingulate cortex(anterior part of corpus callosum) is responsible to sustain autonomic arousal. it is also responsible for empathy, decision making.

So, it is very important to understand that fear and courage as a emotion 2 shades of same feeling but different in expression.

Courage is consciously overcome to feeling of scared or threatening.

Fear as an emotion regulated by a mygdala (hypothalamus) and PNE axis, while courage is regulated by different part of brain that is subgenual anterior cingulate cortex.

Human body vibrate in fear with 19Hz frequency while in courage with 852hz frequency.

So, it is very important to be aware about this emotion during pregnancy. Only will power can shift entire paradigm of two different shades of same emotion.

Let's understand what is courage in spiritual terms?

Spiritually courage defines as a Uproot fear from within by forceful concentration and shifting consciousness to the absolute peace within.

Journey of courage starts with accepting truth without any conflict, accepting the truth about self and our existence.

Courage is another name of DARE TO BE WISE. Many times, it happens people take decision on bases of what other think about, but that is not wisdome.

To be wise means follow your inner voice that, what is to be needed in that particular situation without any hesitation or inner conflict.

Courage defines as a right action on right time.

Practice of courage during pregnancy will bring your child to inner wisdom.

It is purely mothers will that whether she wants to vibrate her body with frequency of fear (19HZ) or with frequency of courage (852Hz) during her pregnancy.

Compassion

639 Hz frequency

Before we understand emotion of compassion first, we will learn about sympathy and empathy, because meaning of words is used interchangeably but there is different meaning.

So, lets understand it…

Sympathy is noun that means feeling of pity and sorrow for someone else's misfortune.

Sympathy is at level of thought; person only think about it. Doesn't have strong feeling.

Empathy is noun

the ability to understand and share the feelings of another.

Empath person experience same feeling, or pain of others.

Being empath means putting your leg in someone's shoes.

Compassion takes empathy and sympathy a step further.

When you are compassionate, you recognize that the person is in pain (i.e., sympathy)or you feel the pain of another (i.e., empathy) and then you do your best possible efforts to reduce the person's suffering from that situation.

So, compassionate I will describe your sympathy and empathy on action level.

Compassionate person not only think and feel but has a will, drive and healthy motive to take action to reduce others pain and discomfort.

Compassionate person vibrates with 639 Hz frequency.

Physiologically there is increased levels of oxytocin

strongly increase feelings of trust, calm, safety, generosity, and connectedness,and facilitates the ability to feel warmth and compassion for ourselves.

Oxytocin is released in a variety of social situations, including when a mother breastfeeds her child, when parents interact with their young children, or when someone gives or receives a soft, tender hug or caress.

research suggest, subgenual anterior cingulated cortex is activated during scanning of brain on empath participants.

Human brain is complex structure, autonomic nervous system responsible to conduct psycho neuro endocrinology.

Let's understand compassion as a spirituality....

Compassion increase sense of responsibility in person, by becoming more aware of other's sufferings.

Feeling of compassion is rainbow bridge from one heart to other. The heart's electrical field is about 60 times greater in amplitude that the electrical activity generated by the brain.

Neuron of autonomic nervous system get fired with same emotion and radiate same frequency to each and every cells of human body by neurotransmitters.

Compassion is the best human quality of understanding the suffering of others and wanting to do something about it.it helps to find out our real purpose of life.

If your kind words can heal someone's broken heart, it makes huge difference in others life.

Well said by Gandhiji if you want to know yourself, then serve yourself to service others...

As gratitude is basic foundation of all virtue, compassion is garland.

Compassionate is act of being, during pregnancy mother is very closed to her child.

Mother and child bond is natural example of compassionate.

One mother can understand everything about her child without uttering single word.

Or else you can understand this way......like

There are so many homeless children is sleeping at night without having dinner, generally you don't relate them.

But when your child gets to sleep without having dinner at night, that doesn't let you sleep that night....

That is strong feeling of compassion, that vibrates your body with around 639Hz and radiate to all over body.

Practice of compassion during pregnancy enhance magnetic field of heart of mother as well as child.

Peace

600 Hz frequency

Dictionary meaning of peace

Noun: means freedom from disturbance; tranquillity.

a state or period in which there is no war or a war has ended.

Peace is a great energy restore emotions.

In this era achieving state of peace or tranquillity is about impossible. Existing reality of human being is little bit strange than other animals.

Every living creature has some common activities to being survive on this earth. Like eating, drinking, sleeping, reproducing and one day dying.

Other living creature do same activities with full potential, while for human being it generates lots of stress to survive on this earth.

For fulfil primary requirement, human has to pay certain cost at any form.so, it is difficult to achieve this state of emotion.

Let's understand what is it?...

Peace is mental STATE, as I explain you earlier that mental state is changeable. So, to maintain it for a long time it requires efforts, but peace or tranquillity in reality-maintained state by our subconscious neuron by default mechanism.

Tranquillity is totally opposite phenomena of fight and flight response at level of physiology.

Human brain is complex structure, collectively well-balanced level of neurotransmitters like dopamine, serotonin, oxytocin, and endorphins.

Peace is an inner state of well-being and calm. It is also an outer project of promoting nonviolence, conflict resolution, and acceptance by cooperation in the world.

Current era, here I will describe your inner conflict is as a WAR.

It is dangerous war because it is always with self.

Peace strength our inner self, and strong foundation to being with self.

Balance of mind and body at level of mental, physical, and spiritual is defined as an ultimate healthy. Here I mention as equilibrium of inner homoeostasis that is all regulatory mechanism at level of mind, body, and spirit.

When you achieve something, you feel satisfy. Or else when you find everything what you want and u get it, everything that makes you comfortable then you feel satisfied, complete or peaceful.

Generally, when the situation around you is comfortable for your ego and your body, these are the times when you feel peaceful. But peace is not something that happens. Peace is something that always is.

If you are interested in productivity, the first and foremost thing is to create a pleasant basis for yourself, to be peaceful doesn't depend on anything.

Here I will make you understand by narrating one

story.

One day one king invited so many artists in his kingdom and demanded to make art picture which reflect PEACE.

Many artists had participated in that event, finally two different picture selected by king.

One had beautiful art of nature, silent water that reflect entire sky with clouds, trees and surrounding.

Second one has lightning storm, black huge clouds with thunder, chaotic surrounding with one sparrow feeding her two little chicks.

All artists were surprised to see that and finally king selected second picture for giving prize.

On asking about controversy, king replies out of discomfort external environment, sparrow doing her job without reacting it, that is the real meaning of peace.

Giving reaction to any external stimuli makes low down our field of energy, by stimulating fight and flight response of human body.

Being tranquil or peaceful is fundamental thing to be in present moment.

So, always chose peace, or be responsive rather than reactive to maintain your energy field during pregnancy.

Here I mentioned to you about primary positive emotion that every one need to practice during pregnancy.

It has a great impact on child's personality, because as a mind and body are the parts of the same system, that constantly communicate with baby's neural network at multiway and multilevel.

So, pregnancy is important period to shape your child's personality.

Apart from that there are other positive emotions like joy, laughing, happiness, self-worthiness, serenity... etc.

All emotion generates field of energy in different vibration.

Part III

Task v/s Outcome

Third part of this book is practical part.

As we learn general guidance of mind and body in part 1

Implanting positive character to unborn child in womb by practice of positive emotion during pregnancy in part 2

Here I will guide you about practical part of entire garbh sanskar.

This part is very essential to build child's personality in mother's womb, because human nervous system can rewire by doing action.

You may have heard or understand about physical activity in form of exercise, yoga, walking and all, but here I want to make you notice about something else.

First of all, let's understand about ACTION

Dictionary meaning of Action(noun)

The fact or process of doing something, typically to achieve an aim.

Human brain always either try to avoid pain or gain pleasure in each and every task.

To put yourself into action here I will suggest some important points:

Majority we all are guided with wrong information like by doing so and so task we will get so and so result.

Entire society is task oriented.

But here I would suggest that first you must have your outcome, means first you have to focus on what you want then decide task accordingly.

You may aware of this thing that some people can easily achieve their goal, while others struggling for same.

People who are not achieving their goal in a given time they usually change their goal or outcome, and blame on external environment for not finishing it.

Basically, there is a difference of internal force that continuously guide us and motivate for doing something.

This internal force can increase when it rewarded by something while punishment makes it intensity down.

So, behaviors are learned by forming associations with outcomes, but there is strong cognitive reason to perform various action.

Practicing garbh samskara, means to teach your child inside mother womb is one of the important actions of them.

Decide your strong reason to practice this guideline, so that continuously stimulate your inner drive and will power.

Part two of this book I have mention vibrational frequency of primary positive emotions.

You can not raise your frequency at physical level without any action.

Love

So, if you want to implant love in your child, you must have performed it at action level.

It sounds so strange, here I need to mention it specifically because human being is not mean to do any action without any strong reason.

After reading this statement you might have a thought that yes, I performing it everyday and it is true for a while.

Everyone love their partner, parents, children, siblings and family members. But when you closely analyses yourself about it, you realize it, that your heart is vibrates only for close 5-6 persons. You may talk about it for other but you can not able to generate same emotion as I mentioned for that 5-6 persons.

So, at energy level of human body it is not sufficient to radiate same frequency as I mention for emotion

LOVE.

So, what you need to do:

Reminding yourself for this frequency, and make your self aware about your feeling that you need to generate it for all living as well as nonliving thing.

You may have seen in case of children, little girl has a same emotion for her toy doll, or little boy has a for his toy car or else.

Kids are innocent so, they don't have a sense of discrimination whether their toys are living or nonliving object. They just radiate same emotion for that.

Its time to be as innocent like children to vibrate yourself with same frequency.

Show your careful nature in each and every task whatever you doing entire day.

I have observed in my clinical practice that everyone has a different location in our life.

One girl is daughter of her father, sister of her brother, wife of her husband, and mother of her children, apart from this so many playing role of friend, sister in law, aunty etc.

Playing a role is one kind of action for that particular moment or state. Girl can not vibrate with same emotion as playing role of daughter, sister, wife or mother.

All frequencies are different, you can understand easily by your own example in your life.

Make your intention so pure that you easily vibrate with this frequency.

FORGIVENESS:

If you want to implant positive character of forgiveness in your child, first you must forgive yourself.

You must erase your past painful memories without any condition from your mental script.

You must forgive others as well, and after that you must replace this MUST word with WANT.

Command yourself that I WANT to forgive myself and others to write down script for my new life…

Daily routine there are so many things you experience that, that is not according to you always. Forgive those all events, people, situation that hurts you.

Make free yourself at your energy level from this hidden and unseen burden, to vibrate frequency of forgiveness.

COURAGE

Each and every living creature has a fear, fear is a fundamental emotion that generates with all survival measures.

As we learn that fear and courage are two different shades of same emotion but operated by different parts of brain and effects are quite different from each other.

Human body vibrates low frequency under emotion of fear and high frequency with emotion of courage.

For implanting positive character of courage in unborn child, one mother must vibrate with high frequency of courage.

First imagine any situation what you scared most, and overcome that situation at your thought level.

Whether it is possible or impossible for you, but overcome at your thinking level. Subconscious neuron doesn't have any differentiation between imagination and reality.

After that do at least three activities what make you discomfort. Break your comfort zone by doing these activities.

Once you start doing physically more than 90% of subconscious neuron rewired by practice it.

As you know whatever you learnt in your life, like writing, cycling, driving, cooking and so many things required multiple efforts means PRACTICE.

Nobody succeeds in first effort, so it well said that PRACTICE MAKES YOU PERFECT.

So, in this way act of courage is essential to processing information by neuronal pathways in human brain to store in long term memory.

So, take challenge and do at least three activities per day that scared you most.

Gratitude

For vibrating with higher frequency of gratitude, say thank you to each and every living or nonliving things.

It could be anything or anyone.

You yourself, your parents, family, relatives, friends, neighbours, your teachers who have an important role to develop your personality.

Your servants, employees, any person who makes your entire day by fulfilling any service like milk man, vegetable wonder, rickshaw driver, newspaper wander, or else.

Nonliving things like all your material requirements from toothbrush to pillow. Whatever you use in your daily life including food, water, clothes, money, vehicles, or else

All the events in your life whether positive or negative.

Say thank you to nature around you, mother earth, sky, clouds, rain, sun, plants and entire universe.

Make it daily ritual to be grateful with everything.

That generates positive loop of thinking patterns and that stimulates biology by generating neurochemistry in side human body.

I hope practicing gratitude by saying thank you at least five persons in a day is not difficult task or action like fighting with fear...

Compassion

I explain about differentiation of sympathy, empathy and compassion.

Compassion is all about taking action.

Here I will give you one example of compassion.

One day one teacher passing by, form street of Calcutta.

She shows one sick person, she did all the efforts to take that person for treatment from one hospital to other.

But she couldn't save that person, and there was deep voice of intrusion that everyone deserves LIFE.

That motivational inner voice driven her in that way that she built trust for poor person and their all requirements.

She is great example of compassionate person; you

know her very well.

I am talking about mother Teresa; how many teachers do you know who were working with her in Calcutta. Almost no one.

To vibrate with frequency of positive emotion of compassionate, do at least three helps for unknown without any expectations.

We used to help known person, because there is sense of perseverance of our EGO, not in terms of compassion. So, be aware about your activities on that perspective.

PEACE

Peace is not a stage to achieve, it is always there.

This positive emotion vibrates with frequency. Peace is a fundamental force to create success in all the areas in life. Like personal growth, financial growth, healthy relationship, social growth etc.

When we come to that some force is always there then your action about it to maintain that force at highest level.

Take all challenges in your life and maintain peaceful state of mind during pregnancy.

It is very easy to maintain peace when things go according to your way, or you can control so and so thing.

But when situation is against you, then your test start that how to maintain your inner programming of mind to control your neurochemistry.

All biochemical changes have a positive intension inside body, because body doesn't know how to be ill.

Human body always tries to maintain internal homoeostasis. Whether you labeled as a high blood pressure, high blood sugar, uric acid diathesis, or vitamin deficiency.

Biochemistry doesn't have capacity to change without your signals of central nervous system. Human central nervous system is operated on bases of perceptions.

So, here I will give some points to reframe your perception.

If situation is in favor to you there is nothing to do, but if it is against you then you need to reframe it to regain your peaceful mindset.

Here there is a list of questions to ask yourself for reframing your perception to maintain peace within yourself.

1. What have I learnt from this situation?

Learning some lesson means to gain something

When human brain perceives to gain something immediately our regrets getting down.

2. What is to be done to solve this problem?

Replace your why to how-Why it is happening to me? replaced by how can I solve it?

Rather than being victim, start being productive and creative in terms of problem solver.

3. What should not be repeated?

Find out your mistakes, don't repeat it

If one solution is not applicable to solve your problem shift to other.

So, these are some sets of questions to reframe your perception.

You can do it by your own way too.

But important action is reframing perception.

Part IV

AFFIRMATIONS

This is also practical part of this book, because for taking right and appropriate action there must be stimulation of neural network for so and so action.

Human nervous system memory stores in form of bites, same as computer. This stored memory has different components.

Like, bright and clear image, sound with good tone, and feeling.

Here I will guide about sound. Every day there are lots of sound ringing at our mental script. If you are aware about your self so closely, you will be noticed that there is a sound of each and every thought.

Here I describe is as an affirmation for implanting positive characteristic in unborn child during pregnancy.

Every action has a definitely precursor sound to

stimulate the neural network.

So, I consider as an affirmation are part of that action process.

Positive affirmations are strong pillar of healthy and successful life.

Research suggest, in human brain neural pathways are increased when people practice self-affirmation tasks.

These neural pathways are basic block to chain one perception to other, and forms neural network.

This neural network may form as functionally or structurally, this is known as a neuroplasticity; this way human brain can rewire anytime.

Here I will go through all positive statement that is affirmations to connect with your child during pregnancy.

Love:

I love myself and my child.

I deserve to receive love from everyone in my life.

I make free myself to radiate the energy of warmth and care surrounding me.

I love my family, nature and entire universe.

Every day I am becoming best version of myself.

Love is powerful emotion to connect myself with others.

I always choose to love unconditionally.

Talk to your child during pregnancy

My child is lovable.

My heart is always open for radiate the energy of love.

I am blessed with loving relationship my life and you are one of them.

I see love everywhere; I feel love everywhere.

I always radiate pure and unconditional love.

I receive love in abundance.

Play these positive statements at your mental script with repeating continuously. Along with it do practical task as I mentioned in part three for vibrating frequency with love.

Forgiveness:

I forgive myself and others as well.

I forgive my each and every part of body.

I make free myself from past, that time has gone.

I am enjoying my present with fully potential.

I have value of my time. I am enjoying each and every moment.

I am willing to move forward.

I perceive my past as a best learning for me.

Forgiveness gives freedom to myself.

Everyone is right in their place.

There is nothing like right and wrong.

Life is all about learning from everything.

Forgiveness built inner strength.

Forgiveness is the first step to move forward.

I forgive all people, situation and events in my life, because it means to be happened for a while; that time is passed away.

With each breath out I release my past regrets, and I forgive my self.

Play these positive statements at your mental script with repeating continuously. Along with it do practical task as I mentioned in part three for vibrating frequency with forgiveness.

Courage:

I choose to be courageous all time.

Do now or never.

I am enough capable to solve my problems.

I have all the resources within me.

Dare to be wise.

I choose to walk like a lion rather than be in crowd.

I am ready to take my responsibilities.

I can serve others without any expectations.

I am rich with courageous energy.

I see opportunity in each and every problem.

I know how to make stepping stone of my barriers.

I can stand on my feet without any support.

I breath courage.

I am healthy, young and energetic.

Every day my mental and physical capacities are increasing.

I am calm and positive in each and every situation.

I chose to take responsibiltiy of my surrounding.

I am productive and problem solver.

Play these positive statements at your mental script with repeating continuously. Along with it do practical task as I mentioned in part three for vibrating frequency with courage.

Gratitude:

Gratitude is transcending of all other emotions. Affirm yourself by following positive statements.

I am thankful to everything in my life.

I thank to all people around me.

I thank to entire nature and universe.

I thank to my parents and all teachers.

I realise that everything happens for a purpose, I thank to all the events and situation in my life.

Nature has selected me to nurture this beautiful life.

I thank my baby to give me wonderful opportunity for motherhood.

I thank to air,water, food,fire, and all the elements of my existence in this universe.

I thank to all people who is responsible to make my entire day.

I thank to all materials which give me comfort life.

I thank to my five senses through which I can able to sense this beautiful world.

I choose to be happy forever.

I am thankful to be part of universe and its mechanism.

I blessed with friends and family.

I thank to all my mistake that taught me great lesson to learning.

Play these positive statements at your mental script with repeating continuously. Along with it do practical task as I mentioned in part three for vibrating frequency with gratitude

Compassion:

I choose to be human.

I can feel other's emotion.

I open my heart to connect with others

I choose love, wisdom and compassion.

I like to serve others.

I am satisfied to feeling worth by helping others.

I am sensitive to needs of others.

I radiate compassion everywhere.

I am treating myself as well as others with care and compassion.

I am deserving compassion from others too.

I am free to exchange my energy with universe.

I appreciate nature around me that teach me how to be serve others without any expectations.

Play these positive statements at your mental script with repeating continuously. Along with it do practical task as I mentioned in part three for vibrating frequency with compassion.

Peace:

I am free to let go my anxiety and hesitation.

I am safe and calm

I choose to be peaceful forever.

Peacefulness is reflecting in my thought, action, and behaviours.

I radiate peace wherever I go.

I am always surrounded by peaceful energy.

I attract peaceful people in my life.

I nurture my self as a great source of peace.

I am comfortable with everything.

I choose to be harmonious with nature surrounding me.

I am free to give and receive love, warmth and peacefulness.

I am secure and I can make others secure as well. Play these positive statements at your mental script with repeating continuously. Along with it do practical task as I mentioned in part three for vibrating frequency with peacefulness.